Diamonds in the Snow

Rescuing the Senses in the
Aftermath of Breast Cancer

Maureen Hogan Lutz

For Melissa,
Thanks for all
your help
with best wishes, Sandy
Maureen Hogan Lutz
October 2012

Diamonds in the Snow:
Rescuing the Senses in the Aftermath of Breast Cancer

First Printing – February 2010

Copyright © 2010 Maureen Hogan Lutz

This book is based on the personal experiences
of the author and select colleagues who have
been affected by breast cancer.
It is in no way intended to serve as scientific doctrine.

ISBN: 978-0-615-34797-4

Published by: Pendulum Communications LLC

Printed in the United States of America
The Country Press, Inc.
Middleboro, MA

For Ellen, Becky and Kristina

"Use your eyes as if tomorrow you would be stricken blind. Hear the music of voices, the song of the bird, the mighty strains of an orchestra, as if you would be stricken deaf tomorrow. Touch each object as if tomorrow your tactile sense would fail. Smell the perfume of the flowers, taste with relish each morsel, as if tomorrow you could never smell and taste again. Make the most of every sense; glory in all the facets of pleasure and beauty which the world reveals to you."

Helen Keller
Three Days to See
Atlantic Monthly, January 1933

Preface

Can rejuvenating the senses really help reclaim an overall sense of well-being? The answer is as individual as is every breast cancer story. The pace of physical healing is affected by many factors including pre-surgical fitness, the extent of surgery, and whether chemotherapy and radiation were part of treatment. Emotional recovery is just as complicated. Some women struggle in the aftermath with a sense of isolation, bouts of depression, anger and anxiety. What works to help one woman reclaim herself may not work for another.

If we at least acknowledge that there is another transition period from patient to survivor we will have taken a step in the right direction. A deliberate effort to rejuvenate our senses after battling breast cancer reminds us that sensation is a precious gift. Transforming negative thoughts into positive ones is not just an emotional remedy—it is a path forward. There is so much energy to be gleaned from optimism.

I proved this to myself after I was diagnosed with breast cancer and struggled through recovery from a mastectomy. Gradually, the idea came to me that if I could share the challenges that I encountered, others might have a more manageable recovery. The result was the Necessities Bag. It incorporated my thoughts and insights, along with a collection of *necessary* supplies, like lip balm, bandages, cotton undershirts, and a hand-made comfort pillow.

With the help of the surgeons and nurses in my own community of Fairfield County, Connecticut, the Necessities Bag has become a must-have for mastectomy patients.

Diamonds in the Snow was written for women who battled breast cancer and are looking for light at the end of the tunnel. I have received hundreds and hundreds of heartfelt letters from bag recipients who shared their stories, expressed appreciation, and offered to join the effort to change the way women manage breast surgery.

The experience of Necessities was so personally rewarding, it became my road to recovery. Just as I discovered that positive action is a way forward, so too did others.

This book is dedicated to three extraordinary women— breast cancer survivors and Necessities Bag advocates. Ellen Mack of Sacramento started the very first Necessities affiliate, followed by Becky Christensen in Wisconsin, and Kristina Alderice in Indiana. Affiliates continue to spring up across the country, but these women were the pioneers. They understood that the essence of the Necessities Bag is the powerful woman to woman connection. Ellen, Becky, and Kristina are real life examples of women turning a negative into a positive to help themselves and others.

I am grateful to my surgeon, Dr. David Passaretti, who offered guidance and encouragement when I presented him with my idea for the Necessities Bag. Nurses Sally Cascella, Michele Speer, Jan Larkin, Elspeth Knill-Selby, Joanne Ballerini, Leslie Handelman, and countless other dedicated professionals in the field of cancer care, personally distribute Necessities Bags. What would I do without them?

The support and encouragement from family and friends made this book possible. My sister Patricia Bittner helped me when creativity stalled; she inspires me in ways I cannot adequately express. Colleen Brown, my steadfast and talented friend shaped the manuscript into a finished product. There are so many others who keep me energized, including Mary Collins, Carol Schneider, Marti Fischer, Marie DeSalvo, Karen Spencer, Rebecca Boyle, Pat Gerner and Rosemary Strimavicius.

Nothing I try to accomplish is ever possible without my husband Peter who has sustained me through thick and thin with unwavering devotion. He guides me with his intelligence, compassion and insight into human nature. Kristen and Peter, my fascinating children who grew up to be my friends, were the gentle, persistent force encouraging my writing. I am me because of their love.

Maureen Hogan Lutz

Introduction

It sounded like gusts of a hurricane. I crossed to the window and looked out. An overnight snowstorm had blanketed the lawn and iced the trees. Branches, naked and rigid with winter, swayed and groaned as the sunrise brought warmth, and leftover storm winds buffeted the crystal coating. With each new gust, ice exploded off the branches and plunged downward with a mighty whoosh.

I rushed outside, squinting as my eyes adjusted to the sunlight splintering through the yellow pines that framed the hilltop. The morning air breathed fireplace smoke and pine sap. My hands flew up over my ears in defense of another thunderous burst of ice shards which covered the landscape and sparkled like diamonds in the snow. An exclamation escaped from the back of my throat and a trail of breath slid across my lips, vanishing into fathoms of air laden with the indescribable scent of a miracle. Later that day, I learned that I had breast cancer.

In the months that followed, there was no delight in sight, sound, taste, scent, and touch. My ears had to absorb what I did not want to hear. I lost my taste for morning coffee. Narcotics dulled the pain sensors of my skin. My eyes became accustomed to periods of dark shadows and distressing images in the mirror.

A breast cancer diagnosis marks the beginning of sensory cocooning. Our lives revolve around a calendar of doctor visits,

1

surgical schedules, and for some women, weeks and months of radiation and chemotherapy. *Aftermath* begins when we hear the words "You're done," as if we are a cake in the oven springing back when pricked. Consciously resetting our sensory triggers is a simple strategy to help us hold it together when we have to come to terms with what has been called the "new normal."

"It is like being on the other side of a fence," one survivor explained. "At some point you have to accept that you will never get back to where you were."

Unlike the treatment period, recovery roads have fewer signposts and no scale of distance. Yet loved ones want to be relieved of their worry and quickly pin on the "survivor" label, unaware that the internal struggle to understand, to come to terms, to find a new center of gravity, to look back over the fence and let go, has just begun. In all fairness, they have had a rough time of it too, offering a hand to hold and an arm to lean on, while fighting to keep fear and frustration from their expression and tone. Helplessness permeates the sidelines as time moves agonizingly slowly for loved ones during surgery. Afterward in the recovery room, they have to confront the sight of an ashen face shrouded in sheets.

Being thrust into premature survivorland has many issues, not the least of which is meeting expectations – our own as well as those of others. Let's be honest. Popular culture focuses on amazing "survivor" stories. Breast cancer patients often get caught up in the notion to become new and improved. We have to stop denying ourselves, seek adventure, get out of a bad relationship and pretend we love our new short hair. We should write poetry, take up yoga, engage in rigorous exercise, go on a diet, become a vegetarian, eat organic, run in a marathon, bike the French countryside — and write a book about all of the above. Breast cancer experiences are different and unique to each of us; so, too, is recovery.

Simultaneous to my mastectomy, I underwent reconstruction that used stomach tissue to rebuild my breast. When I was pronounced "done," I signed up for yoga and found most of the postures difficult, if not impossible, because of stomach muscle disruption and overall body realignment. I left the class near tears. What I did not need at that point was an activity that made me feel like a failure. Recovery from major breast cancer surgery defies the "day by day" standard of healing. Time increments are stretched. Month-to-month worked for me, but in some cases, women use yearly anniversaries to mark progress. Filling those increments by reinvigorating the senses supports us in a way that may not be immediately evident, but eventually something will occur to make us recognize the value of this endeavor—which is exactly what happened to me.

The stress of multiple breast reconstruction surgeries caused havoc on every part of my body, changed my posture and altered the way I walked. I found myself stepping gingerly, moving tentatively, and stumbling often.

One day, I lost my balance in a supermarket parking lot. Down to the pavement I went; hand, arm, and hip absorbing the impact on the side of my body most affected by surgery. I lay there, curled up like an injured bird, head bent toward its wing and feathers pulled round. My mind raced. Had I done any damage to my breast? Was my arm broken? My range of motion was still not fully restored and a cast would be a major setback. Would a broken arm cause the onset of lymphedema?

This could not be happening, I told myself, not after all I had been through.

A voice interrupted the *woe is me* moment. A young mother holding a toddler was offering to help me stand. Through a tearful outburst, the woman learned all about my breast cancer surgeries and fears of a broken arm. Her little boy gawked at the crazy lady before him.

As it turned out, my breast was fine, my arm was not broken, the scrapes healed, but humiliation prevented me from shopping at that store for a long time.

A few months into my "aftermath," I planned a special day in Manhattan. I boarded a train in Connecticut for Grand Central Terminal. Along the way, accompanied by the sound of the rails and passenger chatter, I gazed out the window as the suburban landscape retreated and brick and stone took over, only to disappear when we were swallowed up in a tunnel and chugged underground for the last leg of the journey.

Sultry air engulfed me as I emerged from the train and stepped onto the platform. In the cathedral-like terminal, I crossed the marble floor beneath the vivid blue barrel-vaulted ceiling dotted with glittering lights.

I headed for a lunch date with a friend at Saks Fifth Avenue where gigantic floral arrangements arched over the aisles of polished wood and glass, sprinkled with exotic scents and filled with glittering jewels. I paused at a display of designer handbags to run my hand over the soft leather. In the mirrored panels of the crisscrossing escalators, I eyed myself all the way to the eighth floor café and a table next to a large window overlooking Rockefeller Center. After a delicious salad, a glass of chilled wine, and a length of great conversation, I said goodbye to my friend.

My step was light and joyful as if I had new batteries in my shoes. A block from Saks, I stumbled on a dip in the sidewalk. Down I went, sliding across the cement, scraping my right hand and sending a shock wave through my arm and hip. It was a replay of the supermarket fall, only this time there was no overwhelming sense of pain, stupidity, angst, or panic.

I got to my feet with the help of an outstretched hand offered by a man who barely broke his stride. This was New York after all and I, too, continued on, rejecting humiliation and mentally willing away the stinging sensation spreading across my palm, hip and knee.

On the way home, I contemplated my fall and realized that how I think I feel can actually affect me physically. In giving my senses attention, I believe that the pleasurable moments leading up to the second fall had somehow insulated me against pain and embarrassment. Filling my mind with new sensory experiences had pushed out some of the bad things that had the power to transform me into an injured bird.

There are many amazing stories about people using their senses to overcome handicaps. Helen Keller is the quintessential example. Blind and deaf from a childhood illness, her sense of touch was so keen that she merely had to put her fingers on someone's lips to understand what they were saying. Her remarkable life spanned nearly nine decades, during which she remapped the boundaries of the senses.

Author Sarah Ban Breathnach (*Romancing the Ordinary*) experienced sensory disorientation after suffering a head injury in a freak accident. Her vision was blurred and sensitive to light. She could not smell or taste. The slightest touch was painful and the senses that she had taken for granted became strangers. She calls it her "senseless period" and describes how it felt when her senses miraculously returned, "I was stunned and ashamed at my appalling lack of appreciation for what had been right under my nose. My new life as a passionate sensuist was about to begin."

A *sensuist* revels in sensory experiences and lives a life of intense engagement with the natural world. A physical or emotional trauma can weaken that connection. By concentrating on sense-impressions, we allow our mind to move in a natural sequence from one thing to another. Just like meditation, massage, or yoga, sensual rejuvenation is a way to enlist our own resources to relieve stress, move in a positive direction away from the cancer scenario, and give ourselves a break. This is within our comprehension and grasp. The resources are right at our fingertips, under our nose, on the tip of our tongue, within earshot, and in plain sight.

Rejuvenation starts with a closer look at the miracle that is our body. This in itself is a positive step in recovering from the trauma of breast cancer and perhaps for some, a deeply felt sense of body betrayal.

This book is a journey through the senses. I hope it will prompt you to take time to reconsider the senses and reflect upon how they so powerfully enrich your daily life.

The simple sensory exercises offered in this book will hopefully help you on your road *back*. Sensory metaphors are meant to tweak your poetic imagination about describing experiences for which there are no easy words.

Having some basic knowledge about our five senses is eye-opening and can only add to our appreciation of them. For me, the process of writing this book was the path to self-reconciliation. I hope reading it will point you in the same direction.

We Touch

Chapter One

Touch

I was taking a shower one morning a few weeks following my mastectomy and instinctively turned my chest away from the spray. As the water spread across my back creating a blanket of warmth, I gathered it around me, crossing my hands over my chest, fingering the imaginary edges of my comfort. My mind conjured the image of a rain cloud filling a mountain lake until it overflowed to begin a journey over rocks, forming waterfalls, spilling and pooling into rivers and reservoirs and, eventually, the pipes that led to my shower. With a tilt of my head, a rhapsody of gurgling notes rushed by my ear. I released my hands to cup the rivulets cascading off my scarred breast. When the shower ended, I stood for a long while in the vapor of my musings, reluctant to re-emerge into my reality.

Of all the senses, touch was the most acute loss for me. The mammogram squeezed and the doctor probed. During surgery, anesthesia kept me unaware of the surgeon's cut. Narcotics blocked pain signals to my brain, yet my skin sizzled as if hit by a lightning bolt. Even the touch of a feather would have been too much to bear. An itch below the skin surface under the ribcage was maddening. My reconstructed breast had the sensation of having no sensation. It took me a long time just to enjoy a hug since my torso instinctively repelled the embrace. I became touch-starved.

After a year of multiple surgeries (two lumpectomies, a mastectomy and reconstruction), I found myself floundering mentally and physically. The pressure of the survivor label got to me. Failed attempts at physical therapies, like yoga or other so-called mild exercise, left me frustrated and defeated. Even something as harmless as a spa facial sparked a flashback of "going under."

What I needed was a strategy that I could manage at my own pace and infuse me with a feeling of success. I admit that I was reluctant to participate in a support group or an on-line chat with other breast cancer patients. I had withdrawn into myself.

For some women who have a difficult time regaining their psychological equilibrium, there is nothing wrong with seeking a counselor or joining a support group. Post traumatic stress disorder, most often associated with soldiers in combat, applies to many other traumatic experiences. Breast cancer is a battle that wounds deeply in ways that only those who have been through it can understand. It was only when recognizing how much my senses had cocooned that I decided to try my own attempt at rebirth. I relied on instinct in rethinking my sensory world.

Hold onto that thought...

Metaphors provide visualization for how we think, feel, understand, and impart information. They help us describe a powerful experience, like *diamonds in the snow*. All of us, not just poets, speak in metaphors whether we realize it or not. They make our thoughts more vivid and interesting and help structure our perceptions and understanding. Our language is drenched with touch metaphors. *Keep in touch. A pinch of salt.*

There's a touch of spring in the air. You touched me with your kindness.

Unlike the other four senses, touch is the most social because it instigates physical interaction with others. Reactions throughout the world to touching and being touched vary. The Italians and Greeks are the most touching. The French kiss on both cheeks in greeting. In Arab nations, it is acceptable for men to put their arms around each other and hug in public. I've read that Mexicans have a saying: "A child who is not touched will be unlucky." The presence or absence of touch is felt in all aspects of our lives.

In the late 19th century, the *American Journal of Psychology* deemed *touch* the mother of all senses. It sustains us, provides information, and gives us comfort and pleasure. When we are born, we emerge from the dark, warm, safety of the womb into a big open space and are immediately disoriented. Little hands flailing, we instinctively reach out to make sense of our new world. Displaced from the protected environment of our mother's body, we need to be held, cuddled, and stroked. Touching is almost as important as food to a newborn as they absorb tenderness all over their body.

A young child's brain is incredibly fast at analyzing and absorbing the pain and pleasure messages it receives through touch. As a little girl I remember being fascinated by our toaster and the black wire that connected it to the wall. One day while my mother was busy in another room, I pushed a chair up to the counter and pulled out the black wire. My curious little finger went straight into the socket. Not only did I let out a horrific scream, I am sure my hair stood up on end.

Comfortable in my skin...

Imagine a coat constructed of a miracle fabric that has the ability to mend itself, shape us, hold everything together, keep our body at just the right temperature, and provide the foundation for our touch sense. This miracle coat is our skin.

The skin is made up of three layers: the epidermis, dermis, and subcutaneous layer. Each plays an important role in housing our sweat glands, nerve endings, blood vessels, and hair follicles.

The visible layer is called the epidermis. It consists of dead cells that slough off. Some of this sloughing is invisible and occurring constantly, but the visible flaking of dry skin is a familiar bodily function. The under layer, however, is where the real action is.

Our brain registers pain and pleasure through a complex conduit of receptors located in the second layer of our skin. Each time we experience a touch, the lever is struck, like a telegraph beeping a message along transmitters inside our bodies, sending sparks across the roadways and junctions to our brain. We know if a bug is crawling up our leg even before we can see it. Our skin alerts us to danger through pressure and temperature. It informs and educates us through the ability to differentiate surfaces. This is how we can exist safely in our physical environment. Life would be pure chaos if we did not possess tactile discernment.

Touch and go...

The power of touch lies not just in the physical sensation, but it allows us to experience texture and transmit knowledge. The raised dot system known as Braille gives blind people the ability to read with their fingertips. Our fingers can distinguish between smooth and rough, between hard and soft. Touch is so efficient that we can be informed merely by the degree of pressure we apply. An airy touch is usually nurturing and affectionate, while heavy touch stimulates different nerve endings and might even be a warning of danger. Our touch pressure is a powerful indicator of how we feel.

According to new research published in the Journal of Neuroscience in 2009, people who have smaller fingers have a finer sense of touch. Tinier digits likely have more closely spaced sensory receptors, the authors concluded. This finding explains why women tend to have better dexterity than men, because women on average have smaller fingers.

Touch receptors in our bodies have the ability to stop responding to certain sensations or they would exhaust us. Imagine if the pain of electric shock did not subside. If our body is cold, we slip on a sweater, cover ourselves with a blanket, or just turn up the heat. If we are hot, layers of clothes are removed. Discomfort at a higher level is pain, which we are now asked by our doctors to describe by assigning a number from one to ten, with ten being most intense. Pain can be sharp, dull, shooting, or throbbing. It can be an ache or a cramp. Some pain signals travel faster than others. A prick to our finger is recorded quicker than a cut on our knee.

In an article written for *American Magazine* in June 1929, Helen Keller wrote. "I think people do not usually realize what an extensive apparatus the sense of touch is. Every particle of the skin is a feeler which touches and is touched and gives contact, which enables the mind to draw conclusions."

All thoughts, ideas, imaginings, and decisions are formed in our brain. Looking at an object may allow us to take measure of it, but only through touch do we complete the image for our mind's eye. We can observe objects and revel in their beauty, uniqueness, color, size, shape, but through touch we make a physical connection.

What is so remarkable about the sense of touch is that while our other four senses are located in specific parts of the body, the touch sense is found all over. Humans need to touch and feel for physical comfort and mental health. People live without sight, hearing, speech, smell, but when the sense of touch is lost or disrupted, the ability to think clearly is jeopardized.

High five...

On certain areas of our bodies, touch registers in a generality of sensation. Take an object that has an irregular surface like a portable telephone. Touch the key pad to the shin or forearm. The ridges of the key pad do not stand out, but exist as part of a whole based on the sensation that is registered on that part of our body. When fingers come in contact with the key pad, the ridges and separateness are evident. Our brain, with its knowledge of the number sequence, can combine with touch, enabling us to dial someone without even looking.

Touching and being touched is a way to communicate without speech and draws upon a rich vocabulary through which we give and receive love, protection, appreciation and validation. *A pat on the back. A squeeze of the hand. A touch of the shoulder. A tap on the arm.* Touch receptors also measure impulses generated through negative touch like anger, hate, and intimidation.

Our hands occupy the largest territory in the cortex because millions of receptors are concentrated in our palms and fingertips. A light fingertip stroke over the palm of our hand elicits a sensation that is joyful, erotic, and pleasurable, but can become irritating because of the intensity of the stimulation. Our thumb may be the shortest digit, but it is the most versatile and can touch every single finger facing it.

Touch not only allows us to experience texture, it transmits love and reassurance. Holding hands is an emotional lifeline. Handclasps and handshakes are associated with good faith, greeting, and affection. Our hand is a complex instrument that can flex, bend, grip, point, stretch and soothe. We use it to soothe others as well as ourselves. If we have a headache, we apply pressure to our temples with our fingertips. When our stomach hurts, we rub the ache. We nurture ourselves with touch all the time, but now we need those instinctive impulses to re-learn our personal landscape.

By filling your mind with sensory delight, imagine you are pushing out the bad recollections associated with the breast cancer experience. Simple exercises for the rejuvenation of your touch-sense easily fit into your everyday routine. *Feel* the texture of your shampoo, the bar of soap, dish detergent, coffee grinds that you brush off your counter, the edges of your kitchen table, the warmth of your morning cup of coffee. Put lipstick on slowly, very slowly. Let your tongue swirl around the cavern of your mouth along your teeth and the soft underside of your lips. Walk barefoot on a grass lawn, a cement sidewalk, a sandy beach. Let the contrasts register in your brain.

Fragrance is the single most common trait people associate with a perfect rose, yet to touch a rose is to truly understand its perfection. Liquid silk is how I describe the feeling, using two words that normally do not go together but form a delightful conclusion that the mind cannot help but embrace.

Sexual activity after breast cancer surgery and treatment can be problematic emotionally as well as physically. This is just another "loss" in the negative narrative of breast cancer. How a woman feels about her body affects how she responds to intimacy. The breast looks and feels different. There may be scarring. Reconstruction alters size and shape. A tattooed areola is a reminder of what is gone forever. Regardless of the extent of surgery or the effects of radiation, there is often chest numbness, hypersensitivity, pain, soreness. Even if physical change is minimal, many women acknowledge an altered sense of self.

Touch exercises may seem a baby step in regaining sexual health, but it is one way of relearning responses to outward stimulation. Loving gestures that sustained us through the breast cancer experience are as powerful as physical passion. Once your mind is open to the power of sensory stimulation, a "rebirth" of your sexual persona, new and improved, may be easier to achieve than you realize.

In seeking renewed sexual function after breast cancer, there is evidence to suggest that sensitive touching is the key. Our earliest erotic experiences may have been in semi-public situations such as a parked car, under the boardwalk, or a darkened movie theater. Lovers holding hands, touching thighs under a table, resting a head on a shoulder, is a way to be affectionate and intimate while fully clothed.

Being touched through clothes can sometimes titillate more than being touched naked in bed. In sensuality workshops, participants practice touching with fabrics, like chiffon. Feathers are especially effective in arousing shivers of delight.

Being lightly and delicately touched in such ways can introduce a variety of stimuli that our physiology craves.

In Auguste Rodin's famous sculpture, *The Kiss* (1898), two naked lovers coil into each other. The woman wraps an arm sensually around the man's neck, while he touches her bare hip. She kisses him from below as she falls slowly to the supine. The blatant display of erotic vertigo is breathtaking.

Kisses can be torrid, wild, elaborate, furtive, sweet, or delicate. The exchange of scents, tastes, and textures may only involve a small movement of the lips, but human lips have a thin layer of skin and are densely populated with sensory neurons. Combined with the neurons in our tongue and mouth, the act can set off delightful sensations, intense emotions and physical reactions.

Sensually speaking, kisses can be barely audible, like the rustling of silk or a breeze in the air. In parting, kisses squeak, pop, or make a soft whoosh, culminating in a sigh or exclamation of delight. The kiss has long emblemized the alchemy of love. It awakened Sleeping Beauty and transformed frogs into princes. We kiss objects in superstition looking for good fortune. Dice are kissed for luck, and tourists in Ireland lean down to kiss the Blarney Stone. Mothers kiss their children's scrapes to "make it better."

The kiss has been the subject of endless scientific discussion delving into the complexities of the act and conjecture on how lips may have evolved first for food and later for speech. The quest to unmask the secrets of a kiss and its relation to passion and love will no doubt continue. The mystery and power of the kiss, however, is a gift to humankind. Explore, enjoy and exercise your sense of touch through your amazing lips.

Mirror image...

Here's how touch sensors can enhance the mental image of our face that we take from the mirror. Starting with the index fingers and beginning at the center of the forehead, move the hands downward and away from each other. The thumbs automatically come together at the chin and our hands lay naturally over our cheeks. The pinky fingers go up to trace the shape of our nose. The ring fingers reach to the feel the contour of the eye sockets. Middle fingers stroke the eyebrows. The hands move downward, then upward behind and over the lobes of the ears.

In the same manner, the fingers can map the geography of the chest. For breast surgery patients, fingers can provide the brain with information about scars, shape, and texture. Completing the mental picture is important to feel comfortable and whole.

If you have a reconstructed breast or breasts, honoring and accepting your new body is an important step in recovery. This may sound trite, but it is the attitude fix that can help you get over the feeling that your body let you down. The bra size you've been wearing for years may not work anymore. Going into a fitting room carrying an armful of sizes and styles is annoying. You may believe that everyone is looking at your chest and that may be true, so you just have to get over it. Each day, do something to care for your body and spirit. Believe that you will find your way to embracing the new you.

Love is sunshine...

Two years into my aftermath, my daughter gave birth to a daughter. Sophie Theresa was less than an hour old when I held her in my arms; a life-defining moment so palpable it created an actual physical sensation. It was as if my entire being was being distilled to the simplicity of spirit and that spirit was flowing through me into her. In that moment, I saw my life going on.

In the months that followed, little Sophie broke down the wall I had built up around my reconstructed breast. At some point, it finally dawned on me that holding her against my chest did not hurt and that I had contrived a new set of reflexes to deflect embraces and hugs. Sophie encircled me in a spell of exquisite and unconditional love that shattered the trepidation I had infused into my recovery. It was a turning point, to say the least. Now my little girl climbs all over me all the time and leaves me breathless with grandmotherly love.

Your turning point will come as well.

Touch Exercises

Touch a window when the sun is beating down;
the glass feels smooth. How does it feel on a cold night?

Walk barefoot on a cement sidewalk,
on a deep piled rug, or on the beach.

Let sand run through your fingers.
Put your finger into a bowl of Jell-O.
Catch raindrops in the palm of your hand.

Trace the edges of a table, a book,
a car fender, or a pair of sunglasses.

Prick your fingertip with a needle.
Touch the needle to the tip of your tongue.

Place the palm of your hand on the
kitchen faucet and alternate running
cold and hot water through it.

Pluck or snip a strand of your hair and run it
through your fingers. Run the strand
across your lips and across your tongue.

Lean your cheek against the bark of a tree.
Feel it with your fingertips.

Experiment with different fabrics
to see if your skin's sensations are affected.

We Hear

Chapter Two

Hear

Breast cancer treatment, whether it is surgery, chemo, or radiation, reeks havoc on our body. It is not just the treatment itself, but the medication prescribed to give us relief from the pain and discomfort. Our senses are dulled so we can cope.

At the point when I no longer needed powerful drugs to get me through the day and night, I was given clearance to drive again. How excited I was! Like a prisoner busting out of jail, I grabbed my car keys. The familiar leather of the driver's seat, molded over the years to my curves, welcomed me back with great affection. It was an early Saturday morning and I headed out to no place in particular, choosing a long stretch of country road to spread my wings.

It had rained during the night and the pavement was still wet and glistening. I rolled down the windows inviting the wind to tousle my hair. My foot pressed and released the gas pedal, navigating the dips and bends. My body happily absorbed the rhythmic undulations and my ears welcomed the playful sound of tires hissing over the wet surface. It suddenly dawned on me that I was making music. Like a conductor lifting a baton, I could elicit different sound qualities with subtle movements of the steering wheel as I passed a dense row of trees or an open expanse of meadow. Boldly accelerating through a leftover puddle, I added crashing cymbals to my impromptu symphony. I felt exhilarated, joyous, and in control.

Singing the blues...

Music captivates us because we are rhythmic creatures. Our breathing, heartbeat and many other body functions have an intrinsic rhythm. Certain music, sounds, words, can invigorate us or calm us; two words, *breast cancer,* launch us into battle.

While every woman handles the diagnosis differently, most will agree that we are at a loss for words. Sometimes the shock and confusion is so profound that even the most competent and calm woman is paralyzed, unable to absorb and process what they are hearing. The fact is that breast cancer is something women prefer not to think about unless they have to. Many initially fumble with questions and concerns when it happens to them. Throughout the entire experience, our ears are assaulted with distressing information. Our voice is choked with emotion. Sensory restoration after a traumatic estrangement is all about self-nurturing. Imagine your senses have been wounded along with your body. First aid is called for.

Perk up your ears...

Sound is simply about quivering molecules of air. The movement of any object, large or small, disrupts air molecules and sends a wave of sound to our ears. They pick up sounds and translate this information to our brain. The human hearing system is based solely on physical movement, while our sense of smell, taste and vision all involve chemical reactions.

Our ears are extraordinary organs. They contain the three smallest bones in our body; the hammer, the anvil and the stirrup. The terms themselves provide a visual understanding of how they work. What is truly remarkable is that the space they inhabit is only a third of an inch wide and a sixth of an inch deep.

The human eardrum is a stretched membrane, like the skin of a drum. When the sound waves hit the eardrum, it vibrates and the brain interprets these vibrations as sound. After the vibrations hit your eardrum, a chain reaction is set off. Our eardrum, which is smaller and thinner than the nail on our pinky finger, sends the vibrations to the hammer, the anvil and the stirrup. The stirrup passes those vibrations along a coiled tube in the inner ear called the cochlea. Near the top of the cochlea are three loops called the semi-circular canals, which are filled with fluids that move when we move our head. The fluid in the inner ear presses against membranes, which brush tiny hairs that trigger nearby nerve cells. These, in turn, send a message to the brain. Our brain then translates all of that and tells us what we are hearing.

Our ears not only help us hear, they keep us in balance. You know that if you spin around and around, you will feel dizzy. That is because the ear fluids are spinning as well, confusing the brain. An earache occurs when there is excess fluid build-up in the inner ear caused by infection, allergies, or a virus.

In order to duplicate the ear's function, an engineer would have to create a miniscule sound system capable of equalizing a wide range of inputs, along with a mechanical analyzer, a mobile relay, an amplification unit, a mechanism to maintain hydraulic balance and an internal two-way communication system. Wow!

Now that you are totally blown away by all this amazing information, let's move to the music.

You are the sun, I am the moon, you are the words, I am the tune, play me...

This Neil Diamond song is an example of how music flirts with our imagination. It can have remarkable health benefits; it can invigorate and calm. It can help us sleep, or keep us awake. Exercise classes use music to get people moving and their hearts pumping. It can take us to the heights or depths of emotion. It can be persuasive, kindle memories, help us fight depression, and give us joy.

In his book, *Musicophilia: Tales of Music and the Brain*, neurologist and author, Oliver Saks, declares music to be a necessity in his patients' lives, "with a power beyond anything else to restore them to themselves." He believes music occupies more areas of our brain than language does, and that humans are a musical species.

Babies inside the womb can hear the sound of their mother's heartbeat and the grumbling of her stomach. A mother's voice is music to the baby's ears. A fetus can also hear outside noises like a radio blaring or a car door slamming and react with a sudden jerking movement that the mother can feel. It is widely believed that if the mother listens to soft music or hums to her baby in the womb, the newborn infant will be calmed by these sounds. Just like music stimulates the adult brain, it stimulates the infant's brain to recognize different tones and pitches.

A musical note, just like life sounds, is a displacement of molecules in the air, picked up by our ears and interpreted by our brain. Remarkably, human beings understand and respond to music without actually having to learn it.

Music is universal. The new catchword, "world music" is a way to define all that is not American and recognize the influence of the world's cultures. National Geographic's website, www.nationalgeographic.com, now has a *music* section with an A-Z listing from the familiar Calypso and Reggae to the lesser known Senegalese Pop music, considered to be the most cutting-edge hip-hop scene on the African continent.

Sometimes a song will initially capture us because of the beat, but enjoyment is enhanced through lyrics. How often have we sung a favorite tune convinced we knew the words verbatim? My sister Pat recalls belting out the Huey Lewis and The News classic, "The heart of rock and roll is in Cleveland," only to find out the correct lyrics: "The heart of rock and roll is still beating."

The Internet makes it possible to look up lyrics to better appreciate the poetry of song and the cleverness of the songwriter to capture our imagination.

Much of what we experience of the world is with and through language. Poet songwriters are communication sorcerers. Some of Paul Simon's evocative lyrics forever haunt our minds. "...when my eyes were stabbed by the flash of a neon light that split the night, and touched the sounds of silence."

Bob Dylan is one of the first poet-songwriters of the modern pop music era who pushed the envelope of rhyme. In a 2004 *Los Angeles Times* interview with journalist Robert Hilburn, Dylan offers his take on the potential of our hearing sense. "You can go anywhere in daily life and have your ears open and hear something, either something someone says to you or something you hear across the room. If it has resonance, you can use it in a song."

This is exactly what happened to Amanda McBroom, who wrote *The Rose*, made popular by Better Midler. She was listening to her car radio one day and heard a line in a song,

"Your love is like a razor." As she drove, she thought, "I don't agree with the sentiment. I don't think love is like a razor. What, then, do I think love is?" She felt as if someone had opened a window in the top of her head and worlds came pouring in. "I had to keep reciting them to myself as I drove faster and faster towards home, so I wouldn't forget them. I screeched into my driveway, ran into the house, past various bewildered dogs and cats and husband, and sat down at the piano. Ten minutes later, *The Rose* was there."

Music is the sound of our feelings. If we take the time to *listen*, not just as a background to other activities, our minds can be free to wander wherever the music takes us. Music can make us move in rhythm, sing in harmony and clap with joy.

When I was a teenager, my dad put a record player on the kitchen windowsill and half the neighborhood would gather in our little cement backyard for a dance under the summer stars. Whether it was held in front of a garage, a "finished" basement, or a school auditorium, the Saturday night dance was the highlight of our week. *Moving to the music* was second nature to the "twist, stroll, and mashed potato" generation!

Whispering feet of raindrops...

Beyond man-made music, there is the magic and mystery of life's music, the unrelenting wellspring of pure possibility, escalating and undulating as a great symphony.

As children we are aware of it. Wide-eyed and innocent under the spell of unstructured and unmeasured time, we are able to experience the sky from the vantage point of a flower. In adulthood we surrender to the world of our own making, easily paralyzed by bumps in the road.

We *hear* all the time, but do we *listen* to life's music? Hearing is a navigational tool to our brain. Listening is the path to our inner self. Think about the events and experiences that are not necessarily big moments, but quiet, simple, unassuming ones. Listen to the music you make as you prepare dinner; chopping, scraping, stirring, the sound of the electric can opener, a pot boiling over, refrigerator door opening and closing, setting dishes on the table.

In the 2007 movie, *August Rush*, a young boy in search of his parents discovers his innate ability to make music by listening to the sounds of the outside world...the clattering of an elevated train, the swish of a broom, leaves rustling underfoot.

Awareness of the symphonies that surround us can happen in deliberate moments of contemplation. They can also rise up unexpectedly, as happened to me when riding in my car.

Turning to nature is another way of listening to earth's symphonic quality; standing in the rain, tending a buzzing garden, welcoming a breeze coming through a window.

Verlyn Klinkenborg, an editorial writer for the *New York Times*, is gifted at describing nature's events. His column entitled "How Thunder Sounds" resonates in my brain with every thunderstorm I encounter.

"There is blundering beyond the tree line," he writes. "Soon the tuberous blunderheads trundle over the horizon; they begin to *wampum, wampum, wampum* until at last they're *vrooming* nearby, just down the valley."

Have you ever *listened* to a thunderstorm or were you running around the house closing windows, shutting out the rain, wind, lightning, and explosive sound of thunder?

Life's music is all around us; there to enrich life and bring us delight. So pull in the reins of hurry and listen with your heart.

Speaking of which...

While our ears are the listening device, speech is how we communicate. Humans speak by opening our mouth and forcing air from our lungs into the larynx, our voice box, and then through an opening between our vocal cords, which vibrate.

Throughout our breast cancer experience, most of our conversation focused on the disease. In the aftermath, the word *cancer* stubbornly clings to our lips. Some women seek out counseling or talk with others who have been through it. There are those who will close the door and say it's over, but buried emotions can erupt years down the road.

Speaking and writing are the tools we have to communicate thoughts. In speaking, we have the ability to use tone, volume, pitch, facial expression, and direct interaction with the listener. Writing, however, can be more challenging without these visual aids.

How do we adequately express the troubling questions that still plague us, the anger over what transpired, the fear of recurrence, or reconciliation with our body? A cancer diagnosis may bring a profound life change, but consider this: you might begin to cherish every morning as a new beginning to the rest of your life.

Sing your own song...

If you need to write your cancer story, do it, even if you will be the only one to read it. Better yet, reach inside for a story you have always wanted to tell; a story that will make you happy, make you laugh, or make you appreciate your life.

Throughout our lives we tell and we listen. We share memories and anecdotes with lovers, spouses, friends, children and grandchildren, like the time mom shoved an old piano out the back door, or the crazy kid on our block who would often jump out his bedroom window rather than use the door.

We hear stories about the struggles and triumphs of ancestors we never knew. We embrace memories of holidays and birthdays. We remember the color of our first car and the thrill of our first kiss. Cherished stories and memories collect inside us like rainwater in a reservoir. We need only draw upon them to quench our thirst, wash away our tears, and flood our hearts with joy.

Remembering is one thing, but putting words on paper can be intimidating. If you have something you wish to share before it bursts inside you, begin by pretending you are telling someone a story or composing a letter. If you are more comfortable wrapping your truth in fiction, choose a familiar place as the backdrop where the sights, sounds, smells and textures are ingrained in you. Draw upon recollections of characters you have encountered in your life, like my quirky art teacher who wore a gold cuff on the upper part of her arm. Write what you know.

Our stories validate our lives and enrich those who will come after us. If you want to learn more about the craft of writing, take a class in an adult evening program at the local school. Seek out a writing circle that welcomes newcomers. Once you pick up your pen or put your fingers to the keyboard, be prepared to take the plunge into the reservoir.

Train whistle...

We often think of scent as the most powerful link to a memory; sound can be just as haunting.

Several years ago, I accompanied my mother on an overnight train trip from Florida to New York. The superliner bedroom was smaller than I expected, and Mom was much slower getting around than I wanted to admit.

Mom and I settled into a comfortable routine. When we were not staring out the window, we played card games, did word puzzles, and read. Eventually we rocked and rolled our way to the dining car. Mom expected "Chicken ala King" to be on the menu. We shared a table and stories with a Jersey woman named Evelyn, and Ann from Iowa. Dinner was great. Mom had chicken, minus the king.

When we returned to our compartment, it had been transformed with upper and lower sleeping berths. I looked up at the harness that hung from the ceiling that was supposed to keep me from crashing to the floor and I burst into laughter. Mom joined in and we laughed until our sides hurt.

After changing into night clothes, bumping butts and elbows, I settled into my berth just as the train whistle blew. Mom was tucked in her little bunk beneath me.

"It's eerie," she said. "It makes me think of North Carolina when I was there with your father during the war."

Her voice sounded so small as she continued.

"One Sunday morning in church we heard a train whistle. All the fellows turned their heads to the sound. Everyone was homesick."

Her wistful musing touched me deeply. I fell asleep with a picture in my mind of a church full of soldiers in a town not far from the train tracks we were riding. I thought of my parents as young newlyweds making memories in the face of an uncertain future.

Through the night the train whistled continuously, the haunting sound weaving itself into my dreams. I imagined the whistle had trailing ribbon streamers whipping memories in the wind, brushing the treetops, and leaving threads of color along the way.

The morning sunrise was a quiet one, no riotous explosions, just a gentle awakening to the day. Mom was breathing quietly in the berth below. A fine and delicate haze hung in the air, softer than smoke and dryer than fog, its luminous vapor like a mysterious bridge between night and day.

I hoped that my mother would remember the trip with fondness. As for me, I would never again hear a train whistle without picturing soldiers in a tiny church longing for home.

Exercises for the Ear

Sit at an open window and identify aloud the
sounds that you hear.

Sing in the shower.

Listen to the sound you make when eating
something crunchy.

Identify the sounds of a summer evening.

Listen for birdsong at dawn and count the
different species you hear.

Recite a rhyming poem out loud.

Say aloud words that sound like what they
mean: *hiss, whisper, thump, fluff.*

Ask your doctor if you can listen to your
heartbeat through a stethoscope.

Tune your car radio to a music station
other than your usual selection.

Visit a playground and listen to the
laughter of children.

Look up the words to favorite songs to see if
you are hearing them correctly.

We Taste

Chapter Three

Taste

During my bedridden stage of recovery, I got hooked on the Food Network— in particular, Ina Garten, or as she is known by the name of her television show, *The Barefoot Contessa*. I wrote down recipes, made shopping lists, and dreamed of returning to my kitchen. My mind devoured Contessa's roasted pepper and goat cheese sandwiches, shrimp bisque, guacamole salad, loin of pork with fennel, seared tuna with mango chutney, coconut cake and chocolate sorbet.

Ironically at the time, my taste buds had shut down. The medications—anesthesia from my surgery, antibiotics, and pain killers—as well as emotional and physical fatigue, robbed me of my taste for food and drink, even the cherished morning cup of coffee. The only thing I wanted was Jell-O. Contessa gave me something to look forward to.

Her philosophy centered on filling the home with great smells from the kitchen, which she called the heartbeat of the house. I am not sure why I became so fixated on food when I was not able to face dinner. Maybe I wanted to put the experience of breast cancer behind me, and reset the mood of the house to where it would once again be, as Contessa says, "a place to gather you up in its arms and give you strength to keep fighting dragons."

Sour note...

Patients with cancer may experience altered taste perception as a result of their treatment. The affect on taste is usually temporary and relates to changes in the taste buds. Some patients complain of a constant metallic taste that makes eating unpleasant, while others claim certain foods are too sweet or too bitter.

Once we regain our sense of taste, we often want to "treat" ourselves with foods we missed during our tasteless period. Who cares if we might want more than one dish of ice cream!

Taste buds are sensory organs and play the most important part in helping us enjoy the many flavors of food. Our tongue and mouth are covered with thousands of tiny taste buds. When we eat, the saliva in our mouth breaks down our food and causes the taste bud receptor cells to send messages through sensory nerves to our brain. There is evidence that taste buds are less sensitive in older adults due to the natural aging process along with the ingestion of prescription medicines. Taste buds wear out every week to 10 days and our body replaces them. This rejuvenation happens less frequently as we age, so it takes a more intense taste to produce the same level of sensation we remember.

Taste is a social sense because we like to share meals with family and friends in celebration of an event, to mark a holiday, or gather around the dining room table to talk about the day's events.

Comfort food...

While we love to eat, we eat to live. We also view food to have nurturing qualities when we are not feeling well. Chicken soup, for example, has been a popular remedy for the common cold for ages because the steam from chicken soup may open up congested noses and throats.

When I came home from the hospital after my surgery, friends far and wide would show up with food; from complete dinners, to decadent desserts. Just like chicken soup, the food that was delivered to my doorstep was a palpable gesture of caring—my friends were showing their love and concern. Talk about soul food!

In recovery from sickness or surgery it is not uncommon to look for "comfort food." Much of it is connected to our early years when many of us lived on mom's casseroles and stews.

I remember Sunday dinners of roast beef, mashed potatoes, oodles of gravy, corn, and buttered bread. Sometimes we would have a guest. My mother's friend Marie arrived carrying three white bakery boxes tied like a tower with that wonderful red and white striped string. Inside might be a chocolate cake, a cherry pie or apple strudel, an assortment of pastries oozing cream, or cookies laden with chocolate, nuts or sticky jelly.

These days the traditional heavy family dinner might only take place on a holiday. Otherwise, we eat a lighter diet and consume more fresh fruits and vegetables, which are available year round. Our busy lifestyles often lead us to rely on packaged and take-out foods. My grandmother would be horrified!

Something to chew on...
We all taste differently. Some of us are sensitive to bitter tastes, while others can tolerate hot chili peppers. Allowing food to linger in our mouth, roll around on our tongue, and chew slowly is called *savoring*. A food's flavor includes its texture, smell, temperature, color and spices. Purveyors of fast

food understand this, and rely on food engineers and ad agencies to create and market meals—whether healthy or not—that seduce as many of our senses as possible. Think about that the next time you are tempted to stop at McDonalds.

Much evidence suggests that if a person truly needs a certain nutrient, like salt, body wisdom will produce a craving. We have all had cravings. A pregnant woman might crave ice cream because her baby needs calcium. When we are under stress, something sweet can provide our bodies with endorphins, which is the brain's natural painkiller. That's when we hunger for those chocolate chip cookies or a box of Juicy Fruits.

How many tastes could a taste bud taste.....

If asked, most of us would reply: sweet, sour, salty, bitter. But there is a fifth taste that many of us do not know about: Umami. Both the word and the concept are Japanese. *Umami* is hard to translate but some English language equivalents are *savory, pungent*, and *meaty*.

Thousands of years ago, Greek philosopher Democritus concluded that the act of chewing food crumbles it into little bits and those bits break up into four basic shapes. When something tastes sweet, it is because the bits are round and large. Salty is isosceles triangle bits on your tongue, bitter is spherical, smooth, and small, while sour is large, but rough, angular and not spherical.

When taste buds were discovered in the 19th century, tongue cells under a microscope looked like little keyholes into which bits of food might fit, and the idea persisted that there were four different keyhole shapes, reaffirming the number of taste buds to be four.

According to Robert Krulwich, Science Correspondent for National Public Radio (NPR), in the late 1800s, a chemist named Kikunae Ikeda was enjoying a bowl of dashi, a classic Japanese soup made from seaweed. Dashi was used by Japanese cooks as a stock for all kinds of recipes. Intrigued by the unusual taste, which was not salty, sour, sweet, or bitter, Ikeda went into his lab for answers. He concluded that when the glutamate molecule, which is found in most living things, breaks apart, it becomes L-glutamate (MSG) and that is when things get *delicious*. This can happen through cooking, aging, fermentation, or ripening. Ikeda decided to call this taste "umami," which means "delicious" or "yummy" in Japanese.

A century after Ikeda made his discovery, a new generation of scientists took a closer look at the human tongue and discovered Ikeda was correct - there is a fifth taste. Humans do have receptors for L-glutamate and when something is really, really yummy in a non-sweet, sour, bitter or salty way, it is umami.

A taste of honey...

Taste drives our appetite. We like the taste of sugar because we have an absolute requirement for carbohydrates. We get cravings for salt because we must have sodium chloride in our diet. Bitter and sour cause avoidance reactions because most poisons are bitter and spoiling food can be sour. We have an absolute need for protein, and amino acids are the building blocks for proteins, so the "new" taste umami, which is the meaty, savory taste, drives our appetite for amino acids. Bacon really hits our umami receptors because it is a rich source of amino acids.

Some people eat particular foods not just for their taste, but for their *feel,* like raw clams. Different cultures offer different tastes and we are so fortunate now to have these available to us at our supermarkets; foods like hummus, made from chick peas, a Middle Eastern favorite, the hot spices of Mexico, fresh ginger to use in Chinese dishes. There are Asian grocery stores and multi-cultural delicatessens in most cities and towns, as well as shops for vegetarian or kosher food. Restaurants offer an array of cuisines including Italian, Chinese, Vietnamese, Thai, Indian, Malaysian, Turkish, Italian, Japanese, Russian, French, and of course, Mexican.

Our taste buds enjoy experimentation, but they can also be affected by the most mundane of activities, like brushing our teeth. The detergent in the toothpaste breaks down fat and grease, and the chemicals in toothpaste cause a sour taste that can linger. The next time you drink a glass of orange juice soon after brushing your teeth, take notice that the juice tastes bitter.

Tasty tidbits...

In 1982, just in time for Mother's Day, "The Silver Palate Cookbook" made its debut. Written by two working mothers, it urged and guided millions of home cooks to try new and exciting recipes such as wild mushroom soup, baked Brie, raspberry-vinaigrette, and *pesto, pesto, pesto!* It became one of the most influential cookbooks of the century, selling millions of copies, and reflected America's budding interest in quality cooking and "gourmet" ingredients like capers, tarragon, and balsamic. The impact of *Silver Palate* was to take the snobbery out of gourmet food. It was a by-product of the women's movement, a middlebrow cookbook promoting blueberry chutney, pâté maison, and poppy-seed dressing. It was tailored to a working woman's world: easy brunches, stew suppers, and unfancy, but delicious, desserts.

Today the Food Network has taken home cooking and entertaining to a whole other level. Millions of households tune in nationwide to gain culinary knowledge from a charismatic cast of celebrity chefs. The programs have themes ranging from how to make quick, healthy meals to throwing exotic dinner parties. The shows are entertaining and so visual you can almost *taste* what you see on the screen.

A foodie is what a foodie does...

Just like "The Silver Palate Cookbook" made "middlebrow" the new catch-word for an accomplished cook, "foodie" replaced "gourmet" as the accepted term for someone with an ardent or refined interest in food. The term "gourmet" became synonymous with snobs who ate only at restaurants serving pâté.

To be a foodie is not only to like food, but to be actively interested in it. Just as a good student will have a thirst for knowledge, a foodie wants to learn about food. A foodie will never answer the question "What are you eating" with "I don't know." Foodies know what they like, and why they like it. They want to enjoy flavorful food all of the time.

In your aftermath, think of yourself as a foodie—someone who not only wants food for nourishment, but for enjoyment. Experiment with new herbs and spices. Use whole leaves of basil, cilantro and mint as part of your salad and throw in a handful of raisins and nuts for texture. Consider herbal teas to sauté fish and vegetables. Check out the multitude of vinegars now available in the supermarket; raspberry, tarragon, white balsamic. They add flavor but virtually no calories. Learn to love fresh-squeezed lemons and limes instead of the bottled juices. There is no comparison, especially when you can add their zest to baked goods and sauces. Think *sensation* with every morsel that passes your lips.

Nothing chocolate...nothing gained...

It melts in your mouth. It contains fat—that's no surprise. It has a rich, creamy consistency that also transmits flavor perfectly. It also has a melting point that is slightly lower than the average human body temperature, which gives you that melt-in-your-mouth feeling every time you pop a piece in your mouth. This melting feeling is often described as a true moment of ecstasy.

The origins of this heavenly confection can be traced to the tropical rainforests of the Americas where cacao tree, pronounced *kah kow*, was discovered 2,000 years ago. The first people known to have made chocolate from cocoa beans were the natives of Mexico and Central America. These cultures, including the Maya and Aztec, mixed ground cacao seeds with various seasonings to make a spicy, frothy drink. Later, the Spanish conquistadors brought the seeds back home to Spain, where spices were added. The drink's popularity spread throughout Europe, but the transformation from drink to confectionery did not begin until the Swiss produced the first eating chocolate in the early nineteenth century.

It is often suggested that women crave chocolate more often than men do. Women are habitually given chocolate as birthday and Valentine's Day presents. In our culture, chocolate is thought of as a romantic gift. It's outside the realm of mundane, day-to-day food, reserved for special occasions— and, for women especially, it's associated with love and romance. That could be another reason why women particularly love chocolate: deep down, it makes them feel loved, cared for, and pampered.

According to a scientific studies, chocolate contains chemicals called uploads. Uploads are also found in opium and they serve to dull pain and give a feeling of well-being to people who ingest them. People who eat chocolate produce natural opiates in their brains that soothe their nerves and make them feel good.

The caffeine and sugars in chocolate raise the red flag of guilt, guilt, guilt. Our *aftermath* should not be about guilt in any form. Moderation is the key. If you do indulge, avoid the nut clusters and choose a nice piece of solid dark chocolate over milk chocolate because it has natural antioxidants. Chocolate is emotional food, and reconnecting with good emotions is an important step in sensory rejuvenation. It has been said that chocolate can produce a pleasant "high," often equated to the feeling of being in love. Coffee may help us get out of bed in the morning, but chocolate makes it worthwhile.

Taste Exercises

Savor a piece of chocolate melting
on your tongue.

Experiment with new spices in cooking recipes.

Identify the foods you crave under stress.

Have a piece of salami, then a sweet fruit.

Taste test frozen, fresh and canned
string beans, carrots or peas.

Add raisins, walnuts, apples, or pears,
to a lettuce salad.

Use herbal teas to sauté fish or vegetables.

After brushing your teeth, notice the change in
the taste of your morning orange juice.

Try new-to-you foreign food such as
Brazilian cuisine.

Create and sample a cheese smorgasbord.

Purchase a new cookbook.

We Smell

Chapter Four

Smell

I can reach out in the dark and find it on my bedside table. Its shape is more familiar to me than the TV remote or the portable telephone. In an instant, the smooth pump bottle can drop into my palm a soft and silky miracle liquid to massage my dry, weary hands. More than ritual of self-nurturing, it is a memory link to my girlhood when I first became obsessed with the almond scent of Jergens lotion.

At a time when expensive perfumes and luxurious creams were beyond the reach of the middle class, Jergens was the indulgence of women like my mother who claimed it to be a remedy for dishpan hands, all along knowing it was so much more. I discovered it when I was barely tall enough to wash my hands at the kitchen sink, where the bottle perched in all its glory.

The sink itself is a memory. Cast iron with a white porcelain glaze and six sturdy legs, it was actually a double sink; a deep basin for household chores like scrubbing soiled clothes, or bathing a baby, and a smaller basin for dirty dishes. With my chin barely clearing the rounded edge, I would wash my hands then pump the Jergens. In thinking back, I'm sure it was my first experience with the power of scent.

To this day, Jergens can take me on a journey to a simpler time when life revolved around five days on and two days off. When people took walks instead of shopping, visited relatives and brought cake from the bakery, wore their best clothes, and made Sunday dinner a ritual. We rode bicycles with big fat tires and roller skates with steel wheels. Stickball ruled the street, the brick bakery wall served as a handball court, and a basketball hoop hung from every garage. We chalked on the sidewalk, jumped rope with a piece of clothesline, and sold Kool-Aid for two cents on hot summer days. Remembering is fun.

Hold your nose...

From the moment of diagnosis to post-surgical recovery, there is no particular smell that I associate with my breast cancer experience. My smell sense was shut down. Anosmia is the medical term associated with the inability to smell. My temporary anosmia ended when I received a bouquet of mixed flowers encircling three oversized and dramatic white lilies with pink accents and fuzzy orange stems in the center. The scent of the lilies was so overpowering, it felt like cotton clogging my throat. Even if the vase was placed far away from my bedroom, the smell would wash over me like a bad dream. To this day, I still have a problem with lilies.

In her book, *The Natural History of the Senses*, author Diane Ackerman writes, "Smell is the mute sense, the one without words. Lacking a vocabulary, we are left tongue-tied." However, smells do fall into basic categories; minty, musky, fruity, floral, foul, or acrid.

We use familiar words to describe how a scent makes us feel, or compare it to something we can process in our brain. Notice how I described the scent of the lilies – *cotton clogging my throat*, and *like a bad dream*. For a perfume that is a pleasant sensual experience, I might say, *smells like a velvet ribbon*, or *makes me feel sexy*.

While the part of our brain that produces language cannot help us with words to describe a scent, when the brain's memory center is triggered, it has the power to take us across time and distance, just like my Jergens magic carpet.

The nose knows...

The end of our nose is made of cartilage, a flexible tissue that is softer than bone, but firmer than muscle or skin. Press on the end of your nose, and you can make it wiggle. The top part of the nose closest to our eyes is hard because of the bone protecting the inside of our nose. Nostrils are the two openings where air comes in and is separated by the septum. Inside the nostrils hairs trap dust and other large particles.

During deep inhalation, air is sucked up into our nostrils over bony ridges called turbinates. The air travels to millions of receptor neurons that sit on a stamp-size sheet on the roof of the nasal cavity. Millions of odor receptors in the nose bond with odor molecules in a mechanism that resembles a lock and key. That is why some receptors will respond to the smell of cut grass and others will respond to that of freshly baked bread.

Odor recognition occurs primarily on the right side of our brain, the area responsible for emotions, creativity, passion, and drives. Our left side rules logic and impartiality. This might be why we sometimes have trouble articulating a particular odor, since we relate to aromas emotionally rather than logically.

Strike a heart note...

Scent is a pretty powerful thing. You know that you will feel hungry if you smell something wonderful cooking in the oven. Smells have a strong effect on us, so it makes sense to wear a fragrance that makes you feel good.

Throughout history perfumes have reflected society. The first scents were created out of plant and animal extracts. In ancient civilizations they were used in religious ceremonies, in medicines, and as cosmetics and gifts.

Borrowing from music terminology, each individual scent is called a note. Perfume *notes* are what make up that particular scent. Each note makes up a segment of the fragrance unmasking itself at a different time. The perfumes themselves are a skillful blend of top, middle and base notes. Just as a band is made up of several instruments to play that beautiful song, perfume is made up of many notes that make up the fragrance.

Top notes are strongest scents and last the shortest period of time. They are usually citrus or spice based, giving a strong burst of aroma initially but losing their potency just as quickly.

Middle notes are the main scents and are softer and linger. They are generally floral based and sometimes referred to as the *heart* notes.

Base notes are those deep musky aromas that take you back to nature. They are the foundation of the scent and can be blended with middle and top notes.

The word perfume comes from the Latin phrase, "per" meaning "through" and "fumus" meaning smoke. The French later gave the name parfum to the pleasant smells that drift through the air from burning incense.

Scent of a woman...

There is a memorable line uttered by Al Pacino from the 1992 movie *Scent of a Woman* in which he portrayed a blind Army officer.

"Have you ever buried your nose in a mountain of curls... just wanted to go to sleep forever? Or lips... and when they touched yours were like... that first swallow of wine... after you just crossed the desert."

Every woman has her own scent and it does not come from a perfume bottle. Author Sarah Ban Breathnach in her wonderful book, *Romancing the Ordinary*, writes "A woman's scent is a deeply personal bouquet of diet, heredity, hormones, hygiene and health."

Like a fingerprint, we leave our scent on our pillow, in our car, on our clothes. Babies and children have a pure and sweet scent. The scent of a lover's sweat can be intoxicating. People smell a certain way depending on their activities, where they have been, what they were doing. Helen Keller could identify a painter, a cook, a gardener, a new mother swollen with breast milk.

Scent is not simplistic; it is voluminous, like a woman. In each breath, we inhale a complex recipe of aromas that are naturally emitted by our surroundings and the personal environments we create: pillows on our couch, sheets dried outside on a clothesline, flowers we plant in our garden, scents carried on the wind, animals we pet, people we greet, clothes we wear, the earth we stand on. These scents frame our memories and our reality.

Fragrant morning...

People connect certain smells to specific functions. For instance, we associate almond with soft skin but lemon is linked to degreasing. And while we accept pine in floor cleaners, we reject it in fabric softeners. We learn most of our smell responses, but some are inherently repulsive.

How many products in your home contain fragrances you like? Do you buy a lot of scented items? Or do you like things that have no smell? Whatever your preferences, you are attracted or repelled by certain scents. Does fragrance really make a difference to you?

Our mind does not discriminate between a scent and how we should respond to it. Rather, our individual histories, locked within the recesses of our mind, govern our responses and our feelings. This theory, called "learned-odor response," is why the same aroma can affect us each quite differently. A scent that triggers good memories for one person may revisit painful memories for another.

The consequences of our thoughts make it even more important during recovery from breast cancer that we learn to elevate them. Shadowy, negative thoughts get us nowhere. Let them go!

Lavender and lilacs...

Aromatherapy has infused its way into the marketplace and our consciousness. The mention of essential oils can conjure up images of fragrant body-care products, room deodorant, cleaning aids, scented candles, even holistic remedies.

We are acquiring "scent" memories, an aromatic "fingerprint" of the plants they represent. At the cosmetic and perfume counter, we are intrigued and excited by reference to exotics of frankincense, bergamot, lemon verbena, mandarin, and jasmine. Shopping for food and household necessities is now a sensory task. Spices and herbs of clove, black pepper, ginger, cardamom, marjoram, mint, basil, rosemary, and sage cause us to pause and reflect on their flavor, their "scent." We scan labels on our household products for lemon, pine, vanilla and lavender, not for their antibacterial properties, but to create a halo of their fragrance while we clean. No longer content to merely smell, we want to know what we have smelled and how the scent will make us feel.

I am a passionate gardener. If you ask me about favorite scents, I will say the lilacs of early spring, June roses, and the musky mums of fall. Being in my garden slows my pace, and is for me, a daily celebration of nature's aromas. The journey of scent is uniquely personal. Ask a horse lover, for instance, and they might tell you the smell of fresh-cut hay, the warm aroma of their favorite horse in the summertime, or the invigorating tingle of wood shavings in the stall.

Scent memory...

We do not pay much attention to it, but our sense of smell plays host to a variety of odors every day and gives us important information about the world we live in. We know to avoid rotten food and are alerted to danger by the smell of smoke. People can recognize others by their smell. Some mothers claim to know their child's smell.

None of our other senses establishes a memory database quite like scent. Our response is both physical and psychological. Within an instant of smelling an aroma, we can be sent back to the first moment we were introduced to it.

Helen Keller once wrote, "Smell is a potent wizard that

transports us across thousands of miles and all the years we have lived. The odors of fruits waft me to my southern home, to my childhood frolics in the peach orchard. Other odors, instantaneous and fleeting, cause my heart to dilate joyously or contract with remembered grief."

Each of us has a favorite scent, a favorite perfume, a scent that makes us smile, makes us laugh, makes us feel sexy, or reminds us of another time. Think about the scents, the aromas that make you happy, that are uplifting, that trigger fond memories.

Women know how to do things, to make things, to exert effort, but we need to allow ourselves to be aware of the power of our senses to help us find the balance that will help us heal our heart and body. Sometimes the only thing we have the power to change is our mind. Use your senses to become present in the moment, to honor the wisdom, strength and beauty you possess. Remember, you are the author of your thoughts.

Exercises for the Nose

Take a walk and be alert to scents in the air:
cut grass; the sidewalk or street after a rain;
mud; car exhaust.

Notice if your body scent is affected
by what you have eaten.

Describe how a newborn baby smells.

Try a different shampoo.

Visit the perfume counter in the
department store and spritz away!

Light an aromatherapy candle in your
bedroom a few hours before going to bed.

Tuck a fragrant sachet in your
undergarment drawer.

Make your own potpourri.

There are many websites and books about homemade potpourri. Flowers that work well are roses, carnations, marigolds, violets and sunflowers. Use herbs like chamomile, lavender, thyme, sage and rosemary. Also, you can save pine needles from your holiday wreath after it has dried out. Place in a zip lock baggie in the freezer until next holiday season.

We See

Chapter Five

See

Long ago, I fell in love with the inherent mystery and magnificence of the ocean; its song never stopped singing in me. Where else would I go to rejuvenate my senses?

I grabbed my favorite yellow plaid cap, a frivolous purchase because it made me feel like a teenager. The beach I chose could only be accessed by way of a steep staircase that was at least a twenty foot drop. By the time I reached the sand, the rain thickened and a dark cluster of clouds rolled across the sky.

Squinting through the moisture collecting on my eyeglasses, I pulled my cap down lower. I had hoped to search for a lovely shell or a delicate gull feather while enjoying the sound of a gentle ebb tide. Instead the ocean tossed itself and roared, the giant waves crested and ruptured, slamming down to the shore. The wind and waves seemed to shout obscenities as though the sky and earth were battling each other.

My heart pounded thickly as I skirted around haphazard piles of driftwood and tangled seaweed intent on finding a memento to take home, but only broken shells were scattered about. I attempted to dry my glasses, but it was of no use so I tucked them into my pocket, squinting to keep my vision in focus. The sand-laden wind stung my cheeks. I was wet and cold through to my bones.

I picked up my pace, almost breaking into a run, giving up with a huff and stomping away, my windbreaker billowing, up the towering staircase, annoyed with myself for wanting more than it would seem I could have. With a suddenness that startled me, I stopped short. My yellow plaid cap was gone.

Frantically reaching for my glasses, I scanned the beach as I raced down the staircase telling myself it would be easy to find a speck of yellow in the grayness. I tried to retrace my steps, but quickly became disoriented so instead I screamed at the ocean that I would hate it forever for stealing my cap.

As I dragged myself up the stairs, the ocean kept shouting at me. Defiantly my hands went up over my ears. Unbalanced, I tripped on the top step and fell to my knees. The clouds in my mind suddenly shifted and I turned my head back to the horizon.

For too long I had been absorbed in my own hurt, causing my senses to malfunction. The ocean made me see what was right in front of me. The yellow plaid cap was the old me; it was time to turn the page.

Tears on my pillow...

From the moment we wake up in the morning to the time we go to sleep at night, our eyes are working. Everything we look at is sent to our brain for processing and storage. When we look at an object we are actually seeing beams of light bouncing off it and into our eyes. Light rays enter through the cornea, which is a thick, transparent protective layer on the surface of our eye. Then the light passes through our pupil, the iris, which is the colored ring, and changes the size of the pupil depending on the amount of light available. Of course we have all had the experience with a bright light momentarily blinding us until our pupils react. Too much light makes our pupils shrink and vice versa.

Just behind the pupil is the lens and it focuses the image through a jelly-like substance onto the back surface of the eyeball, called the retina. The retina, which is the size of your thumbnail, is filled with approximately 150 million light-sensitive cells called rods and cones. Rods identify shapes and work best in dim light. Cones on the other hand, identify color and work best in bright light.

Both of these types of cells then transmit the information to the brain by way of the optic nerve. The image that is sent to the brain arrives upside down. It is the brain's job to turn the image right side up and then tell us what we are looking at.

Because our eyes are such an important and complex part of our body, they are protected by the eyebrows, eyelids, and lashes. Eyelashes help keep the eyes clean by collecting small dirt and dust particles floating through the air. Eyelids sweep dirt from the surface of the eye and protect it from injury. Our tears constantly bathe the front of the eye to keep it clean and moist.

We associate tears with emotions. *She cried for joy. She wept inconsolably.* Non-emotional tears are the ones that are instigated by eye irritations, for instance, when we chop an onion. Emotional crying produces tears that contain the most proteins. We have all heard the expression that "a good cry" makes us feel better. Well, there might be something to it.

The Greek philosopher Aristotle theorized that crying at a drama cleanses the mind of suppressed emotions by a process call catharsis: the reduction of distress by releasing emotions. Modern research on substances in tears is ongoing because there is reason to think that emotional tears may be important in the maintenance of physical health and emotional balance. *Cry me a River,* but *Don't Cry for Me, Argentina.*

For your eyes only...

You hear, but do you listen? You touch, but do you feel? You look, but do you see? These are questions I encourage you to keep asking yourself. Breast cancer is the beginning of many life changes. We *look* at ourselves differently and I do not mean internally, I am talking about visually.

After my mastectomy, I would deliberately steam up the bathroom mirror with long, hot showers. When I was finally out and about, I was convinced that everyone was staring at my breasts; that people were feeling sorry for me. I started walking with my arms crossed against my chest, shopped for loosely fitted blouses, and collected a wardrobe of vests and cardigan sweaters.

I don't have to tell you that we live in a very breast-oriented society. Breast cancer poses many challenges, particularly in facing how we feel about our altered body, and how we think others now perceive us. Some women join support groups; others turn to a counselor or a girlfriend for their emotional lifeline. No matter how much outside support we receive, or how helpful a role model, there comes a point when we have to look to ourselves and confront the trauma of breast cancer. I am convinced that thinking about our sense of touch and vision as they relate to body image can help move us in a positive direction.

If our eyes are not weary enough from body image issues, the environment that we are thrust into because of diagnosis and treatment is unsettling. Think about all the machines and instruments we faced with trepidation. We had to walk into surgery on our own two feet, and climb on the operating table while our eyes were assaulted with strange objects. In the recovery room, our vision was clouded. And no matter how lovely the infusion area decor, it was what it was. Our eyes absorbed all of these images and sent them back to our brain where they wait to haunt us.

It is time for some new *stuff*.

The eyes have it...

Our eyes are our window to the world around us and the pathway to our sense of wonder. Author Sarah Bath Breathnach describes wonder as "the extravagant state of bliss induced by something new, the strange, astonishing, mysterious, and the unexpected."

What if I told you that today there is a wonder waiting for you? If you blink you might miss it. I remember one occasion when something wondrous took place right before my eyes; fortunately, I did not blink.

The pine tree near my back door was still brushed with snow even though the last storm had passed days before. I was standing at the sink when a flash of blue went past the window. My eyes focused to make sense of what was happening and I realized that a flock of blue jays, perhaps a hundred of them (no kidding) had settled randomly in the evergreen. Blue dashes of color against dark green branches tipped with white made the perfect Christmas tree! It was a miraculous moment beyond my wildest imagination. There was no time to get a camera; my eyes captured the moment for my memory to keep safe.

Wonder is all around us; the hummingbird in the garden, baby birds hatching in a nest tucked in the Christmas wreath we left on our front door too long; fireflies; a flower growing in our garden that we did not plant; a litter of newborn puppies.

Children are often described as having "a look of wonder in their eyes." Of course; they are seeing the world for the first time. A child can be mesmerized by a balloon, a colony of ants smothering a piece of cookie on the ground, or their mother's keys. It is only as we get older that wonders are transformed to humdrum, monotonous and tedious.

There are wondrous things occurring all the time if only we see it that way. Have you ever grown your own tomatoes? The sweetest taste ever! Our car is a wonder of engineering, so is the stereo that fills our home with music, and the internet link that brings the world to our fingertips. If we eliminate the word *mundane* from our thinking, and take a good look around with a renewed appreciation for what is right in front of our eyes, our internal batteries will get a restorative boost.

Open your eyes...

Art stimulates different parts of our brains to make us laugh or cry or experience a whole gamut of emotions in between. Looking at art can provoke reflection, sympathy, inspiration, and even ecstasy.

If it has been a while since you visited an art museum, make plans to go. It is a place that offers ways to deepen our knowledge of history, cultures and artistic practices. Looking at artworks encourages our observational skills and perhaps unleash the artist in you.

I particularly like the impressionist painters of the mid-nineteenth century. At the time they were considered radicals because they broke all the rules. American artist Henry Bacon was quoted as saying "they are afflicted with some hitherto unknown disease of the eye." The reason for skepticism is they gave priority to freely brushed colors instead of a disciplined line of color. Monet, Manet, Degas and others in their group saw the world differently. They found that they could capture the momentary and transient effects of sunlight better by painting *en plein air*. Painting outside in the real world was unheard of. Their scenes of modern life were astonishingly realistic and emphasized vivid overall effects rather than details.

A work of art is incomplete in itself. When we enjoy it, we extend it, improve it, and quite possibly, make it our own. There is only so much an artist can do. Art attains its eternal nirvana only when an onlooker enjoys it as much as the artist did. Art can captivate us because of a mysterious allure. We admire art, yet we may never know why.

Art plays a large part in enriching our lives. I am not just talking about a painting. Art is something that is aesthetically pleasing to us, but it can also be functional. I know women who consider a designer handbag a work of art.

Sisters of the Earth

If you have ever browsed through a library or a bookstore hoping that something would jump out of the shelves and tell you to take it home, then you will understand why I cherish my copy of *Sisters of the Earth, Women's Prose and Poetry About Nature,* Second Edition.

It is a stirring collection from more than a hundred poets and prose writers, including several from the "who's who of literature," such as Emily Dickinson, Willa Catha, and Diane Ackerman, author of *The Natural History of the Senses.* Using the feminine in referring to "Nature," the book is divided into sections of essays and poems that urge us to contemplate the delight we take in *Her*, what is untamed in *Her* and in us, and how *She* heals us.

One of my favorite essays was written by Linda Hogan, the daughter of a Chickasaw father and a white mother, "What Holds the Water, What Holds the Light." She describes a water jar that had been placed on the sink and filled for her: "It was thin clay that smelled of dank earth, the unfired and unshaped land it had once been. In it was rain come dark sky. A cool breeze lived inside the container, the way wind blows from a well that is held in the cupped hands of earth, fed with underground springs and rivers."

This is just one example of how *Sisters* highlights women's special ability to see beauty and significance in the small, and the close-to-home. A butterfly in the garden is a beautiful sight. We all know that the butterfly was once a caterpillar until following some deep, inner knowing, it retreats into the darkness and isolation of a cocoon. In time, as promised by its inner wisdom, it emerges as its true self. The butterfly is a symbol of hope and transformation.

We have to be patient with ourselves as we deal with our own transformation and believe that there is a winged and wonderful self within us.

The mind's eye...

What happens when we look right at something —missing keys, for instance — and fail to see them? Have you ever driven somewhere and then could not recall which route you followed or what you saw along the way? The eyes may not *see* at all when the mind is preoccupied. Our eyes do not exist in isolation. How clearly we see is influenced by much more than only the muscles in and around the eyes. Our ability to see is one of the great evolutionary accomplishments of the human brain, but if our brain is holding onto negative clutter, we will miss a lot of what is happening all around us.

Seventy percent of our sense receptors are in our eyes. Even in low light, such as candlelight or moonlight, we look at the world around us, but sometimes we do not see all there is to see. We are so programmed to making things happen for others, it is time to give ourselves permission to slow down so that we can be open to experience the unexpected surprises that await us.

Exercises for the Eyes

Watch a sunset from beginning to end.

Do a jigsaw puzzle or a word search puzzle.

Get a deck of cards and play solitaire.

Stare at a stationery object for 30 seconds.
Close your eyes. Do you still see the object?

Look at the trunk of a tree, then hone in on the
details; the branches, bark, lesser thick
branches, leaves, even the veins of the leaves.

If you wake during the night, do not turn on a
light; allow your eyes to adjust to the
darkness and navigate your way around.

Search the term *Optical Illusions* on your computer.
Choose a few sites to test your eyes with visually
perceived images that differ from reality.

Try this next time you peel an onion: place a toothpick between
your front teeth and press down. Notice if tightening the
muscles in your face helps to control your tears.

A Rose is a Rose is a Rose

Chapter Six

Sense of Self

When I turned thirteen, Marilyn Monroe was the most famous movie star in the whole world, the sweater girl look was all the rage, and women with large breasts had their pick of men. At least that was the notion I was growing up with.

While most of my friends were beginning to "develop," I was as flat as a pancake. Nevertheless, I begged my mother to buy me a training bra, a little swatch of elasticized fabric that constantly rode up into my armpits. Shedding cotton undershirts for a bra was as monumental as a first kiss. To hurry things up, I mailed away for a breast exerciser advertised in a magazine. Made of two pieces of pink plastic in the shape of a palm and attached by a spring to create tension, the gadget promised to increase bust size with regular use. I stood in front the mirror morning and night pressing palms together and imagining my breasts growing before my eyes.

In my lifetime the female breast evolved from a symbol of nurturing to a sexual ornament and was used to sell everything from cars to magazines. Many women considered their breasts the center of their power as well as a measure of beauty. No one bothered to tell an impressionable young girl that beauty cannot be measured by bra size. My battle with breast cancer taught me that and more. The disease that strikes fear into the heart of every woman is so emotionally devastating because of the belief that we need our breasts like Wonder Woman needs her gold bracelets. After losing a breast to cancer, I had to come to terms with my loss. Reflection revealed to me that while I was fixated on movie stars, the very essence of womanhood was in front of me all along.

Rose Angolia was five years old when she arrived in America in 1898 from Italy. Thirty years later my grandmother was a widow with six children. To keep the family together, she toiled in a garment factory sewing overcoats. Her life was difficult and often frightening, but she conquered poverty and loneliness through sheer determination. She moved in with us when I was six and she was sixty to help care for me and my three siblings. Along with a host of mundane household chores, she taught me how to crochet and sew; I bless her for those skills to this day.

Grandma was fastidious about her personal appearance. Her morning ritual included the donning of a corset, a most complicated garment in her simple wardrobe. Regardless, her breasts were simply soft curves that gave feminine shape to her short, slightly plump body. A hug from Grandma was a tonic for all hurts and problems.

When she died at the age of 81, there was a great emptiness in my life that was difficult to articulate. It was years before I came to realize that what made my grandmother so very special was her entire demeanor. She carried herself with grace, never spoke badly about anyone, never gossiped, and she never said anything that was unnecessary. The air around her was perfume and unbeknown to me, it seeped into my pores. There was not one thing in particular that gave her such aura and incredible power with people. Not breasts. Not gold bracelets. It was everything.

The truth of my own womanhood was revealed when I was diagnosed with breast cancer at the age of 57. I managed to put on a brave front and cloak myself with courageous words, but deep down I wondered how Wonder Woman could survive without her bracelets. Eventually I discovered a secret wellspring inside me, fed by life's experiences and the whisperings of a grandmother. My recovery came through an outreach to others who were facing a similar trauma. Looking back, it was in many ways a remarkable experience. I came to know that there is so much more to being a woman than gold bracelets. I am a composite of my feminine ancestors and the women who taught me, nurtured me, and loved me. A woman's true power lies in her willingness to share her life and use the lessons she has learned to help others. I know this for sure. My grandmother told me so.

Photo on page 71 is Rose Angolia Guerriere

Resources and Further Reading
The factual information about the senses comes from information culled from the following sources:

<u>Websites</u>
National Institutes of Health, Bethesda, MD
http://www.nih.gov

Web MD LLC
http://www.webmd.com

Discovery Communications LLC
http://www.howstuffworks.com

SEDL-Southwest Educational Development Lab
http://www.sedl.org/scimath/pasopartners/senses

Oracle Think Quest Education Foundation: Come to Your Senses
http://www.thinkquest.org/3750

Perfumes.com
http://www.perfumes.com/eng/history.htm

Fieldmuseum.org
http://www.fieldmuseum.org/Chocolate/history.html

<u>Articles</u>
"How Does The Sense Of Smell Work? What Causes A Smell?" April2000. http://health.howstuffworks.com/question139.htm Accessed September 2009.

"Women Tend To Have Better Sense Of Touch Due To Smaller Finger Size." December 2009. Science Daily. http://www.sciencedaily.com/releases/2009/12/091215173017.htm. Accessed December 2009.

"Making Sense of Taste." David V. Smith, Robert Margolshee. Scientific American. March 2001. Accessed July 2009.

"Sweet, Sour, Salty, Bitter . . . and Umami." Krulwich, Robert. November 5, 2007. National Public Radio. http://npr.com. Accessed July 2009.

"What Do Urban Sounds Do To Your Brain?" Barone, Jennifer. July 24, 2009. Discover Magazine. Accessed August 2009.

"Rock's Enigmatic Poet Opens a Long-Private Door." Hilburn, Robert. August 4, 2004. Los Angeles Times. Accessed Dec. 09.

Books

Ackerman, Diane. *A Natural History of the Senses*. Vintage Books. February 1995.

Anderson, Lorraine, Editor. *Sisters of the Earth—Second Edition*. Vintage Books. November 2003.

Breathnach, Sarah Ban. *Romancing the Ordinary— A Year of Simple Splendor*. Scribner. 2002.

Garten, Ina. *Barefoot Contessa Family Style Cookbook*. Clarkson Potter. October 2002.

Keller, Helen. *To Love This Life*. AFB Press. American Foundation for the Blind. 2000.

Lukins, Rosso, and McLaughlin. *The Silver Palate Cookbook*. Workman Publishing Company. 1982.

Matthews, Nancy Mowll. *Mary Cassatt*. Harry Abrams, Inc. in association with Smithsonian Institution. 1987.

Saks, Oliver. *Musicophilia: Tales of Music and the Brain*. Vintage Books. 2007.

Schnipper, Hester Hill. *After Breast Cancer—A Common Sense Guide to Life After Treatment*. Bantam Books. October 2003.

About the Author

Maureen Lutz is the Founder of Necessities, Inc., a non-profit organization that supports women battling breast cancer with the Necessities Bag™— a tote of information and supplies to help manage surgery and recovery from a mastectomy.

Writing has always been her passion, primarily penning fiction. Her writing took a new direction when she was diagnosed with breast cancer in 2005 at the age of 57. After recovering from a mastectomy, she wrote *The Woman to Woman Guide to Prepare for Mastectomy* in which she offered insights about the challenges of recovery. She then assembled what she felt were *necessary* supplies and called it the Necessities Bag.™ Today the Necessities Bag is distributed to thousands of women in eleven states, including Connecticut, where Maureen lives. She and her husband Peter reside in a 100 year old Victorian house, with a picket fence, perennial garden, and welcoming front porch.

Maureen can be reached through her website:

www.maureenhoganlutz.com

For information about the Necessities Bag, log onto:

www.necessitiesbag.org